The Haunting

on

East 27th

A spirit investigation conducted by
William Channing Russel, Esq. in 1862
based on his original journal

Edited by

MICHAEL C. DOOLING

111.　　　　　　My wife informed me this evening
that the Menzies family had been troubled by
strange noises in the house 107 E. 27 the St.
that men's footsteps were heard in the Hall
and ascending the stairs, and walking in
the room overhead; that the front door would
be heard to open and on going to see who
was coming in the rush of a passing person
was perceptible & his steps could be counted
as he ascended the stairs; that at night
the bedroom door would seem to open
and a person would be heard to enter the
room when the door would seem to the
ear to close again; that in these cases there
would be no reality in the opening for that
the door would always be found locked on
the inside; that these nightly footsteps had
been heard by Miss Menzies her Mother &
her niece; that they had so alarmed the
last that after one nights experience she
had refused to sleep upstairs & had come
down into the room of the two others; that
one night the Mother & Miss Menzies had been
alarmed by the falling of the piano stool
in the room above & had set up half the night
in fear of burglars but on the next day
the furniture was found undisturbed &
the windows closed; that it was a constant
frequent occurrence to pass on the stairs what
seemed an invisible person, or to have

First Page from Mr. Russel's Journal

Author's Collection

The Haunting

on

East 27th

A spirit investigation conducted by
William Channing Russel, Esq. in 1862
based on his original journal

Edited by

Michael C. Dooling

The Carrollton Press

MMXIV

First Edition

ISBN # 978-0-9627424-8-4

Printed in the United States of America

Contents

Foreword

It is a most unusual journal about a most peculiar assemblage of circumstances. It was written, quite legibly, by a strong hand with bold strokes and with an excellent command of the English language – undeniable evidence of a confident and educated man. The daily journal was kept by a Mr. William Channing Russel, a respected lawyer residing in the fair city of New York, and recorded the course of his investigation into a series of unusual, I daresay strange, occurrences at a dwelling located at 107 East 27th Street.

Over time, the tattered journal had worked its way from Mr. Russel's hands into my own modest library. It soon found a home amongst my eclectic antiquarian collection, nestled on a shelf somewhere between my books relating to nineteenth century voyages of discovery and my prized seventeenth century tome on witchcraft. It is certainly not the handsomest book in my collection, nor the earliest or most valuable, nor the most historically important. However, it does have the distinct honor of being the most intriguing volume I have acquired to date.

When I first inspected the piece, I had little knowledge of the subject matter contained therein but it quickly grasped my attention. In a manner of speaking, it spoke to me, forcefully telling me I must own it. Upon bringing the manuscript to its new home, I studied it late into the evening hours amidst the historical and literary ghosts that haunt my bookshelves. I soon experienced a distinct chill running the length of my spine. Perhaps it was just the bite of a cold December night penetrating my private sanctum that caused me to seek a change of venue. Perhaps...

Disturbed, though not specifically frightened, I laid down the book and retired to the security of my bedchamber. There, I spent the darkest hours of the remaining night restlessly sleeping in short phrases, punctuated by the creaks and groans of my older dwelling.

With the warming light of day, I again found myself drawn to the spineless leather-bound volume and began to learn more about the case that possessed this Mr. Russel. At her home on East 27th Street, a Miss Menzies had heard strange noises including footsteps noisily going up stairs, an invisible presence rudely brushing past her, furniture mysteriously moving about, doors loudly shutting closed and the sudden appearance of a lone skeletal arm beckoning upward from the floor boards. All this occurred with no apparent natural cause and had greatly frightened the poor woman.

Through word of mouth, Mr. Russel had become aware of the situation and was brought onto the scene to investigate the disturbing events. The course of his investigation swiftly brought Russel into the uncharted haunts of spirit mediums and clairvoyants. They in turn brought messages from a not-too-distant, non-material plane into his own terrestrial sphere, providing a map of sorts for his own voyage of discovery.

I had so many questions I wanted to ask this chap Russel; about the strange events, about his personal views regarding them, about their aftermath. But the cruel and irreversible passage of time has prevented this desire from ever becoming a reality, for the happenings about which he so carefully had written occurred some fifteen decades ago.

To this day, the incidents described herein remain unexplained and the thorough investigation conducted by William C. Russel, Esq. is all that is known of the circumstances surrounding those events. Perhaps others, more insightful than I, will be capable of understanding the true nature of these strange phenomena, for this antiquarian ghost hunter and seeker of spiritual truth is at a loss. So please, if you so desire, immerse yourself in Mr. Russel's tale. And have a warm cardigan nearby, should the need arise.

Michael C. Dooling

Memoranda of Examinations of the phenomena of "Spiritualism"

by

William Channing Russel

November 14, 1862

My wife informed me this evening that the Menzies family had been troubled by strange noises in the house 107 E. 27th St., that men's footsteps were heard in the hall and ascending the stairs, and walking in the room overhead, that the front door would seem to be heard to open and on going to see who was coming in, the rush of a passing person was perceptible & his steps could be counted as he ascended the stairs; that at night the bedroom door would seem to open and a person would be heard to enter the room when the door would seem <u>to the ear</u> to close again; that in these cases there would be no reality in the opening, for that the door would always be found locked on the inside; that these nightly footsteps had been heard by Miss Menzies, her mother & her niece; that they had so alarmed the last that after one night's experience she had refused to sleep upstairs & had come down into the room of the two others; that one night the mother & Miss Menzies had been alarmed by the falling of the piano stool in the room above & had sat up half the night in bed & in fear of burglars; but on the next day the furniture was found undisturbed & the windows closed; that it was a frequent occurrence to pass on the stairs what seemed an invisible person, or to have the sensation that a person was standing by or following; that on one occasion Miss Menzies had walked from sleep in the middle of the night & distinctly seen a skeleton arm stretched from the floor upward; that the sounds were heard by all but that as the niece was timid nothing had been said about them in her presence and her remarks on them had been treated slightingly; that Miss Menzies had begun to think the house was haunted and that these disturbances were attributable to spirits.

I treated the suggestion with derision and argued to my wife that as the three women slept in one room without ventilation and as I knew them to be drinkers of strong tea & of a great deal of it, the apparent noises did not seem to me to be unnatural.

Who are the Menzies?

The family consists of a mother[1] about 78 years old, the widow of an English naval officer, a Purser, of her daughter of about ___ [2] years old, who is by occupation a seamstress; and of a granddaughter, Miss Scobell ___ [3] years old who attends to the housekeeping. They are eminently respectable people, intelligent, industrious, simple, of ordinary education but of varied practical capacities. They are Episcopalians but

---

[1] This refers to Mrs. Rose Menzies, widow of Thomas Menzies.
[2] Her age has been crossed out and is illegible.
[3] Miss Scobell's age has been crossed out and is illegible.

not very religious, rather inclined to superstition, not unmindful of fortune tellers, but moderate in their tone, truthful and honest.

The grandmother receives a pension from the British Government and the daughter has constant employment for her needle in a few families who depend on her weekly visits for their mending and altering. In this way she has been employed for years in my wife's family and since our marriage has usually spent one day in each week in our nursery. She has always been spoken of with the greatest respect and her reputation is in every way unexceptionable. I have never known anything in any degree derogatory to the good report the world gives of her.

In the summer of 1861, the family were invited to occupy part of our house during our absence in the country. Previous to our return, they left and last summer the invitation was again extended to them and they occupied our house until the autumn when about October 20th they left and hired the lower floor and basement & kitchen with one room in the 3d story of the house No. 107 East 27th St.

This house is built with two others on the rear of a lot fronting on the 3d Avenue. It is about 20 feet front by about 25 feet deep, brick & of four stories in height, of the English basement pattern. The kitchen & cellar were, of course, under ground and above them on the ground floor was one room occupying the entire area of the house. Its one rear window opened into a granary and to secure the room from burglars a sheet of zinc had been nailed over that possibility of entrance. Two front windows looked upon the street and the gaslight from the neighboring gas post would shine through the linen curtains at night sufficiently to make objects in the room visible.

All the rest of the house except what I have mentioned was occupied by a school[4] during the day, but at night was unoccupied. The rear window of the 2d story opened into the Granary and was always kept fastened. In the roof is a scuttle door opening down into the large room on the 4th floor but it has always been fastened with a hook and staple and there is no ladder, nor steps leading to it.

MISS. SOPHIA J. RUSSEL

WILL REOPEN HER SCHOOL at 107 East 27th-street, on Monday, the 22d inst. Beside her own class, there will be cla-ses of younger children, under the Kindergarten System, and especial attention will be paid to Calisthenics in both Departments. S32-tf

---

[4] This school was actually run by Russel's daughter and was about to reopen on November 22, 1862. (*Christian Inquirer*, Nov. 15, 1862, p. 3).

November 15, 1862

On hearing the story of the noises, I determined to visit the house & investigate the case. Armed therefore, with a dark lantern and a knife I went up on the evening of the 15th November and took my position in one of the schoolrooms, the one immediately over the sitting room and which seemed to be the favorite resort of the invisible walker. A good fire was soon lighted and I had a long conversation with Miss Menzies in which she detailed the circumstances already alluded to. There could be no doubt as to her sincerity.

She believed that there was an intelligent being who in an invisible state was in the habit of visiting the house. All my suggestions as to want of ventilation, nervousness or imagination were confidently repelled. I threw myself into her humor & professed my entirely willingness to entertain any ghost who might come and she and I orally extended the invitation to the spiritual world. But none came.

She left me about midnight and I continued the watch sometimes reading, sometimes dozing, and at others *arrectis auribus*[5], but always with my knife within reach until about 4 o'clock a.m. Nothing occurred in any wise unusual, and tired & disappointed I left the house as the cocks began to crow and the milk carts to rattle.

---

[5] Latin expression, "with attentive ears."

November 16, 1862

In conversation upon these events with Dr. B. in the course of the day, he unhesitatingly pronounced the disturbance to be spiritual & urged me to procure a medium & try to learn what the spirit wanted and why he made so much trouble.

The unhesitating manner of Dr. B. surprized [*sic*] me. He was the first person whom I had ever heard profess a belief in ghosts. But he did it simply and so confidently that notwithstanding some stories he told me and which I would not believe, I was induced to examine the matter more seriously and from the spiritualist side - I had no faith in spirit manifestations. I had never heard a rap nor seen a table tip, but had never formed my opinion in denial of the truth of manifestations. I had never cared about the matter, had been very averse from it and looked at it more as a phase of mesmerism[6] than of spiritual natures.

About twilight, I again visited the house and saw Miss Menzies. She told me that while I was watching upstairs the night before, the footsteps were distinctly perceptible about her in the bedroom where she was sewing until frightened and tired at 2 ½ a.m. she went to bed. In vain I courted an interview with the intruder, in vain I assured him of my readiness to talk to him – every thing was quiet. Miss Menzies' first knowledge of Spirits happened as she says in this way, using her own words:

"I had always charged these noises on Johnny. I know that he slept in the house & had his meals there

---

[6] A hypnotic state.

and so long as he kept out of my way I did not forbid it. It was hard to turn him adrift before we had found a place for him & I knew that my niece let him in at night & sent him up stairs to sleep. Still, I was a little annoyed by his coming there and told my niece that I knew that the clattering about the house all came from that miserable boy. She denied it and one morning we had quite a dispute about it. I went away quite irritated to Mrs. Howland's to work."

"In the evening I returned home. It was quite late but when I reached the door I felt badly about what had happened between my niece and me in the morning and I stopped in the space between the outer and inner doors. It was Halloween Eve & a beautiful moonlight night. I hesitated about ringing the bell, not knowing what to do about what had passed in the morning. I stood there some time when I heard footsteps coming down stairs & toward the door.

Now, thinks I, I've caught you, supposing that it was Johnny, and I meant to give him a good shaking. But as I waited for him to come out, the door seemed to open but did not open, and the steps came out and passed me to the front stoop. I looked but could see nothing. I stepped out on the stoop but there was nothing there. It was perfectly bright but there was nothing to be seen. I did not know what to make of it and went back to my place between the doors."

"There, the steps came up on to the stoop again & into the house and the door sounded as if it opened and shut. I was perfectly confounded and partially stood and partly crouched where I was for a long time and the same thing was repeated three or four times, the steps coming out of the house passing me and then coming in again and the door sounding as if it opened and shut. I must have been there an hour, till at last, perfectly bewildered, I rang the bell and went in."

Dr. B. said that he had been to 14th St. to see a medium & ask her to go up to the house but that she was ill but would be able to go on Tuesday the 18th. We made an appointment accordingly.

This Johnny was a boy of about 12 years old whom Miss Menzies tried to assist by finding situations for him and, as often as he lost or gave them up, by taking him into her home. But he was a lazy little loafer and she lost all patience with him and forbade his coming near her. Miss Scobell persisted a while longer but finally sent him to the Juvenile Asylum.

November 18, 1862

On coming home, I learned from my wife that Miss Menzies had been working at Mrs. Howland's[7]; that she was so pale & worn that Cornelia enquired particularly about her health, in reply to which Miss Menzies had told her of her late experiences & of last night's especially. She woke, as she said, and saw a man's figure standing at the foot of the bed, that she was able to distinguish his features & the color of his eyes and that the description corresponded exactly to that of old Mr. G. who had died in that room five years ago, in the opinion of Cornelia who knew him well. This statement my wife received from her sister this p.m.

This Mr. Gantion was a French gentleman of 45 to 50 years of age who some years since resided in this same house. He had a wife and a son who taught French and a daughter who gave music lessons. They were very poor and were visited and assisted by the Howland family. The father was ill for a long time and died as I am told in the room now occupied by the Menzies family as their bedroom. The rest of the family then returned to France.

I now feel that something ought to be done to relieve the Menzies family from the distress they were suffering, and called on Dr. Baner. The medium he had expected to employ had gone to Rochester, but he took me to Dr. Gray to whom I stated the case and asked his advice. He told us a story from Cicero about a spirit who haunted a house near Athens until his bones, which were found in the garden, were dug up and respectably buried. The sequel to the story was his

---

[7] Mrs. Cornelia Howland was Mr. Russel's sister-in-law.

advice to procure a medium and have an interview with the deceased and he thought that Mrs. K.[8] might go.

We called on Mrs. K., a lady, light hair and complexion & middle aged - could not go – family opposed to spiritualism – would raise an artery. But would talk to Miss Menzies if she would come there.

Went after Miss Menzies & carried her to Mrs. K's.

She told Miss Menzies that she was a medium, none but a medium can see spirits. She took her hand and explained to her that this man had something very important to be told & wished to say it to her.

"Oh Yes," says Miss M. "He was very anxious to speak."

"Certainly he showed it by his looks didn't he?"

"Oh Yes, he looked convulsed with pain because I would not let him speak to me."

"Yes, of course you saw that he had something on his mind that he wanted to say."

"Oh certainly, he begged me to listen to him – putting out his arms beseechingly as if to say would I only hear him, but I told him that he must not speak to me and I covered my head up in the bedclothes and turned away from him."

"Now if you had only spoken to him, he would have told you something and probably left you, and you would never have seen him again. I think I have an impression of him. He was quite straight – grey eyes large and sunken - florid complexion."

---

[8] Mrs. K. has not been identified.

"Oh yes, very straight and broad shouldered - with grey eyes."

"Not a fat man but a large frame."

"Exactly - a well built man."

"His forehead is wrinkled."

"Oh. I remember distinctly two very deep wrinkles up and down his forehead. They were very marked & when he looked so anxious to speak (he) seemed very deep indeed."

"He has more than a medium mind."

"He was what I call a double-storied man."

"Yes, with quite a high forehead."

"My impression is not very clear but I think I have an idea of him. He died suddenly."

Thus the conversation continued for about an hour and ended in Mrs. K's recommending us to see Henry Gordon[9]. Down we accordingly went to Henry Gordon's, No. ___ Sixth Avenue. "Dr. Henry Gordon" and "Dr. Spooner[10] Dentist" on two tins marked the house. A girl admitted us into the entry on the ground floor. Dr. Gordon was engaged - had a circle tonight - could we see Dr. Spooner - girl will enquire. While we waited, three tremendous raps on the wainscot reminded us that we were on spiritual ground.

---

[9] Henry Gordon was one of the earliest American physical mediums. In February, 1851, he was reportedly one of the first to be levitated and a year later was levitated above a crowd at the New York Conference, floating a distance of some sixty feet. His home address was 66 West 14th St.

[10] Dr. Spooner also resided at 66 West 14th Street.

"Are those raps?" asked I.

"No," said the girl, "that is the grocer fastening up the cellar next door."

Presently, a man of about 40, with quiet features and smooth black hair, came down and was introduced as "Dr. Spooner." We explained our errand & that we had hoped to get Gordon to go up with us. Spooner said that Miss Menzies was a medium & that all that was necessary was that she should recognize and obey the laws of God. "Only feel that you are ready to do as he commands and to receive the light of Jesus into our heart, and all will go well with you."

He would see if he could get an impression of the man & he shut his eyes, leaned back against the wall, folded his hands and looked like a man going to sleep. After the course of a minute he resumed his position, said that he thought he could give Miss Menzies something which would help her & handed her a card which he told her to keep by her and she would probably be secure from annoyance.

Just then, a rich female voice from the story above attracted my attentions. It seemed at first to be that of an elocutionist reciting poetry but on closer attention it proved to be that of a woman making an address. The tones were singularly musical and sympathetic & reminded me of Fanny Kemble's[11].

Dr. Spooner said that it was that of a lady in a trance & asked us to walk up. We did so and found that the front room was filled with men and women, some of the former in military uniforms, all sitting very attentively listening to a

---

[11] Fanny Kemble (1811-1893) was a popular British actress and writer.

vision. The lady in exquisite tones, but miserable grammar, described the troops passing on to the war and their wives & children suffering at home and appealed to the hearts of her audience to admit their claims.

We stood on the outside of the half-open door and through it could discern the audience and an altar. In the middle of the vision a small spare man, of sandy hair, no color, grey listless eyes, some 40 years old passed us in the hall. He was dressed in a frock of white muslin and over his shoulder he wore the American flag. He entered the front room but after a few minutes reappeared in apparently an epileptic fit. He found his way however past us into the back room. After a little while he reappeared dressed in ordinary gentleman's costume of black and was introduced as Mr. Gordon.

He took us into the back room and we began to expect some conversation when, after a moment's absence, he entered from the passage dressed as before in white muslin and apparently in another epileptic fit. His eyes were shut and he walked two or three times up & down the room pacing rather solemnly, then stopped before the mantel clock and pointed to the figure XII. "He is showing you how the spirit walks at 12," said Spooner.

After showing us this sufficiently, G. disappeared again and reappeared in a black silk gown and with a silver baptismal cap in his hand - epilepsy still on him. He advanced towards Miss M. and salutes her with the cap and stretched his arms over her. Then, by an amazing effort, seized a pitcher of about his own size and raising it aloft with his right hand and holding the cup as low as he could reach with his left, he filled it from the pitcher by pouring in a continuous stream and without the loss of a drop. Then with the cup he approached Miss M. & raised the cup in the air as if to pour a libation over her, but considerately only let fall a few drops harmlessly upon the carpet at her feet. "He is baptizing Miss Menzies as a medium," says Spooner.

This done, the priest again left the room & reappeared with a huge vase of artificial flowers in his hands - epilepsy still in the ascendant. The vase he set down on the table near Miss M. and with both hands pushed clouds of imaginary perfume from the artificial flowers towards her. "He is showing her that the spirits will pour out on her light and the fullness of rich gifts," says Spooner.

At the close of this ceremony, the performer disappeared and after a minute reappeared in his usual dress, epilepsy gone but with the appearance of a man utterly exhausted and drained of vital energy. He immediately drew out the table, we stood around it, when twitching with a sort of whoop or chirp he began writing very rapidly on a piece of paper before him.[12]

After writing a few lines, which were frequently interrupted by twitchings, he tossed it with another whoop and a chirp towards us. The writing was as follows:

"I hope you will not leave me dear father. I came here to greet you through this medium. I am your dear little Mary."

---

[12] Many mediums use the technique of automatic writing in which they scribble messages seemingly dictated by a spirit. Sometimes they start by writing gibberish and soon letters, words and complete sentences are formed.

Neither of us recognized this as intended for him or her. But while we were reading it, G. had begun to write again with the same rapidity and after a while jerked and whooped and chirped the paper towards Miss Menzies. It was as follows:

"You are affraid [*sic*] to see me are you? I hope you will talk with me when I come to see you. I love to walk about the house but do not wish to <u>frighten you</u>. Why will you not talk with me? I am a spirit and I am not coming to harm you but will unfold to you much which will make you happy. Do not fear when I come again for I promise you I will not do you any harm."

In this interview two points deserve attention. First, the marked recognition of Miss Menzies as a medium. Second, the pertinency of the second letter to the object of our inquiries - of which I do not believe that Gordon had any idea.

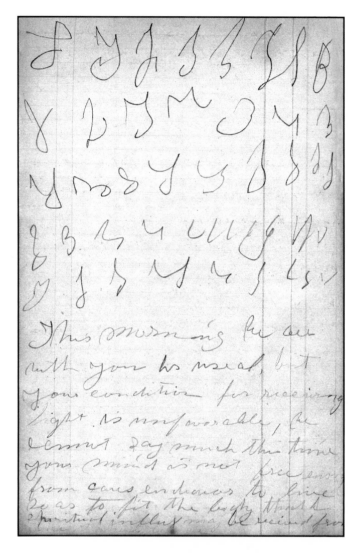

Example of Automatic Writing with False Starts
Unidentified Medium, 1859
Author's Collection

The First & Second Circles

November 20, 1862

Dr. B. called at the house this morning professionally and found me at home. After I had expressed my desire to do something for the Menzies family, he offered to introduce me to a medium whom I might arrange to go to the house this evening. We accordingly jumped into his chaise and rode to the SW corner of 14th St. & 6th Avenue. Mrs. Hayden[13] was at home and we ascended - rooms furnished simply, neatly - Dr. Hayden, the medium's husband, received us. Mrs. H. returned from Rochester last night. Presently she enters - full height - rather large figure - light hair - light eyes - fair complexion - 40 - temperament lymphatic – good, pleasant, honest face.

We left her husband & took her into an adjoining room - there explained our errand and arranged to go up to the house that evening. After laughing over the scene at Gordon's house and talking about him, I asked her if there were any spirits there present who wished to communicate.

"I am sure I do not know," said she, "any better than yourself but we can ask."

---

[13] Mrs. Maria Hayden was influential in the spiritualism movement and the first American medium to visit England in 1852. She was married to William R. Hayden, physician, editor and journalist. In 1853, he started publication of the first spiritualist journal titled *The Spirit World*. They resided at 66 West 14th St.

We then put our hands on the little table around which we were sitting.

"Any body here?" asked Mrs. H.

After a very short pause, Dr. B. said, "There are the raps."

I heard nothing but on putting my hand upon the middle of the table I distinctly felt vibration and heard the sound of three faint raps on the underside. This was my first experience of rapping.

The Doctor took the alphabet[14] and began pointing to the letters in order. When he touched the letter "F," three faint raps were again heard. He then began again and on touching "A" three raps again - the same at "T" and at "H."

"Father?" asks Dr. B.

3 raps replied.

In the very same manner were spelled out the words:

"I AM VERY GLAD TO SPEAK TO YOU."

"Is it for me?" asks Dr. B.

3 raps

"Well I am very glad to hear you speak. Marianna?"

3 raps again.

"I am very glad to speak to you daughter. Something to say to me or to mother?"

3 raps

---

[14] A placard with the alphabet and numbers was used. A member of the circle pointed to the characters until the spirit rapped, gradually spelling out, letter by letter, the message the spirit wanted to convey.

The Doctor then pointed to the letters on the alphabet while I noted those to which the raps seemed to respond. Nothing was said as to the meaning of the message until it was completed and it was apparently entirely fresh to the Dr. when he read it. It was these words:

"I love you dearly and Mama too. Dear little Pet at home is entwining its tender petals around your hearts as did your Marianna, and I am so happy."

The Doctor stated that some two years ago he lost a child named Marianna and that her baby brother at home was the only thing that was filling her place.

I then asked, "Any body for me?" and I thought of Sarah.

Three raps clear and sharp.

"Please give your name or communicate," said Mrs. Hayden.

Three raps as before.

"Will you please answer by the alphabet?" said she.

And again three raps.

We then took the alphabet and the following words were spelled out:

"Brother do let me speak with you," - a long pause - "But to you."

I then took the alphabet and Mrs. Hayden wrote down as the letters were indicated.

It then proceeded as follows without any intermixture of my mind for my attention was too strongly fixed upon the letters and the raps, to catch the meaning:

"Dear Brother do not doubt our power and purpose; we do live, are happy and can bless our earthly friends. We

27

are all together Willie" - the same reason for this as before - "You shall see and hear and know what is now appearing to you a mystery. Robert."

"I have no brother Robert. If you are my brother, give me your name."

"Frank" was then spelled out. "Yes but there is somebody here whom you love a great deal better than me."

Three raps.

Note: "Willie." This was the consequence of my jumping at the conclusion that I was to receive some message about his son and telling Mrs. H. that "Willie" was the word. Probably it would have been "William."

I asked first Mrs. Hayden and then the Dr. to get the name of the person meant. First one tried and then the other, but though they pointed to every letter in the alphabet, no raps came to any. Mrs. Hayden remarked that there must be some strong magnetic influence between my brother and me & handed me the alphabet. I pointed to the letters and very readily the raps spelled out "William." I then said that it was very evident that my mind was operating to produce the raps and urged Mrs. Hayden to try again to get the second name. She tried - pointed to all the letters - no response.

She tried again - no response - and she was in the act of turning the alphabet upside down when the card was thrown down violently and the pencil was grasped strongly and forces as by a spasmodic nervous effort on a piece of blank paper on the table before her. There the pencil twitched and stuck as if guided by a blind impulse to write on the part of somebody not accustomed to do so. It must have struggled for half a minute, Mrs. Hayden all the time laughing and complaining of the powerful grip under which her arm was held, when at length the hand began to move and convulsively traced a word which neither Mrs. Hayden nor Dr. B. seemed able to read but which to me was plainly "Francis."

I then asked if there was any other spirit there who wanted to communicate with me - three gentle raps. I took the alphabet and the raps spelled out "Sarah."[15] I then gave the alphabet to the others and asked them to get my wife's second name. I was thinking of "Jackson," and did not wish my mind to interfere. After some vain efforts, and my saying "Sarah, please give your middle name to Mrs. Hayden," the raps spelled out "Cabot." I then asked:

"Sarah will you meet us at the house in 27th St. this evening?"

Three raps gentle and soft.

"And Frank, you too?"

Three raps sharp and clear.

Thus ended my first sitting with a medium. In the evening, Dr. B., Mr. Haskell and I carried Mrs. Hayden to the house where we with Miss Menzies constituted ourselves a circle. Mrs. Hayden after a pause said, "If the Spirit who visits this house is present will it manifest itself by rapping?"

To this question we waited for a response for a long time. We made ourselves passive - we lowered the light, we were silent, all to no purpose. I was supposed to be too ardent and

---

[15] Sarah Cabot Jackson was Russel's first wife, who died in 1844. Their daughter Sophie lived with Mr. Russel and his second wife.

went off upstairs but with no better result. The question was repeated by different persons but none received an answer.

In the course of our waiting, I said that my wife would be very much interested in the object of our visit - that she would care as much as anyone to have the disturbance abated & we occasionally called on her & my brother not long after in the midst of silence. Mrs. Hayden was forced by apparently some powerful influence to write and having done so she threw me the paper. It ran:

> "Dear dear William we are deeply interested in the object for which you have met - and your urging us to speak will thwart that important object. Please be passive - S. J. R."

At the time this writing commenced I was not thinking of my wife nor brother nor of any other spirit. I was half asleep - very passive. The initials deserve attention for in the morning Mrs. Hayden was informed that my wife's middle name was "Cabot."

After waiting for an hour, we finally gave up all hopes of any communication from the walking spirit and turned our attention to others. After calling for my brother, Mrs. Hayden seemed again to be seized by the arm and taken possession of, on that limb. She complained of the force and of the awkward way in which her fingers had been made to clutch the lead pencil, which made it impossible for her to reach the paper with it until it had, with some difficulty, been pressed through her fingers and she said that it was evident that the spirit was not used to writing through mediums. Finally, after several fruitless attempts at beginning, she wrote rapidly & violently talking to us pretty much all the time as follows:

"My dear Willie,

I am very anxious to have the spirit, who wants so much to communicate with this lady, say what he is so very desirous of doing for he is a friend, nay a relative and it will, when it comes, be of great advantage to this lady, and further she must be passive and let him say what he wishes. He will not harm her but bless her. We have not been able to induce him to manifest at this time as his communication is private and important so that it will be useless to wait for what he wishes to say. For my own part, I am too happy to come to you to say that I am disinterested. I am with dear Sarah and we are all very happy together. I think she will speak to you.

Your affectionate brother Frank

The error of addressing me as "Willie" may have been a repetition of my error in the morning session with this same medium or it may have been the imperfection of the writing which is very rough and more than once omits several letters of a word. On reading this I said, "There is another person whom I would have supposed you would have mentioned as being with you."

Three taps.

"Will you give the name of that person?"

Three taps.

I then asked Dr. B. and Mrs. H. to get the name & said that to prevent my mind from influencing them I would turn my back which I did and only heard what followed. They appeared to be pointing to the letters of the alphabet, but to which letters at any particular moment I could not tell, but they very readily spelled out the letters L U C Y![16]

Considerable conversation there ensued in the course of which Mrs. Hayden was again moved to write. This time the influence was quiet and gentle and the handwriting was delicate and comparatively clear. Mrs. H. continued conversing while writing, though her eye occasionally sought the paper. The writing was as follows:

Dear Dear William,

She is a medium [we had proposed to ask if Miss Menzies were a medium] but as yet in an undeveloped state, so much so as to preclude communication for the present time at least. Yet, if she were to sit for us we could manifest through her - and to you also.

The conditions are so charged that we cannot rap - the spirit who has made those noises in this house has control of the present manifestations so that we can't make definite manifestations by the raps. We will be able to manifest to you hereafter in a decided manner so you may depend upon my coming to you Dear. Lucy says tell William that I am very happy to come to him and we soon (will) be able to communicate with you with the dearest love. I can see him just when I please. [I had been asking whether it was supposed that spirits saw *ad libitum*[17] so that my wife could see Cabot[18]]. With many blessings.

Your affectionate wife,
S.J. R. [19]

---

[16] Possibly a deceased daughter of William and Sarah, though they had another daughter named Lucy who was still alive.

[17] Latin for "at pleasure" or "at will."

[18] William and Sarah's son who was studying at Harvard.

[19] Apparently William's late wife Sarah Jackson Russel.

The setting then broke up and I accompanied Mrs. Hayden to her home where I paid her the price she charged for her services - $5. As we were expressing disappointment at the poor results of our experiment and she said she wished she could find out from my brother the cause, she asked if he were present.

Three raps answered.

Several inquiries then followed. Among other things, I asked:

"Am I right in my suspicion as to who the walking spirit is?" [meaning Gantion]

Three raps.

"Will you give his name?"

Three raps.

The alphabet was then taken up and the name given was "John Ingram."

"Do you mean to say that is the name of the walking spirit?"

Three raps.

"But did you not say that I was right in my suspicions as to who he was?"

Three raps.

"Do you mean to say that I thought the walking spirit was John Ingram?"

Mrs. Hayden was here compelled to write, "Brother there is two."

"Please give the name of the other."

The alphabet being resorted to the raps spelt out the words, "William Young"

"What is the name of the person whom I suppose the walking spirit to be?"

With great difficulty the alphabet stammered out, "Charles Gantion."

"Is he the one she has seen?"

Mrs. Hayden was here again compelled to write:

"Sometimes and then, the others who are so very much interested with the other spirit - this spirit will be that woman's society if she will ask him greatly to her advantage. Do tell her so. Frank."

After some further conversation as to the probable connection between the Spirit and Miss Menzies, the writing continued:

"He was a kind of miser and she is poor, or comparatively so, and that may account for his desiring to speak with her and I very much fear that he will not leave until he has accomplished his purpose. She did see the arm and also the whole man several times [I had spoken to Mrs. Hayden as to the probability of Miss Menzies having seen the skeleton arm]. His death was sudden and untimely - was assisted out of this world - this to yourself remember."

I asked my brother where his son was. The answer was at first "England" but afterward "Jamaica Plain." This ended the evening.

November 21, 1862

Miss Menzies tells Mrs. Russel that last night we were leaving and the carriage wheels had hardly left the curb stone, the steps of the spirit were heard coming down stairs by her as she closed the door after us.

Excerpt from November 20, 1862

35

November 22, 1862

Miss Menzies tells me that she had seen a young girl in the attic, a high spirit who vanished as she entered.

November 23, 1862

Called on the Menzies and attempted by sitting at the table with Miss Menzies & Miss Scobell to establish communication. Sat for an hour. Miss Scobell has heard so much of these noises that she has divined the object of our investigations and her aunt has informed her of the whole. At this interview both women tell me of the effect of the

spirit's steps upon their dog. He crouches on his belly, and whines piteously while if any other steps are heard he barks most independently. No result of the sitting was apparent.

Called on Judge Edmonds.[20] He says these difficulties are common - promises to consult his "friends on the other side" as to the time of meeting there with his daughter.[21]

Judge John W. Edmonds

---

[20] John W. Edmonds was a former New York Supreme Court justice. He became so involved in spiritualism that he stepped down from the bench amidst controversy over his beliefs.
[21] This refers to Edmonds' daughter Laura, a well-known medium. She had the ability, though never educated in them, to speak nine or ten languages when in trance.

November 24, 1862

Judge Edmonds called & said he had been up to the house & talked to the Menzies - made an appointment to meet me there with Miss E. on the 25th at 8 p.m.

November 25, 1862

Called at the Menzies at 8 p.m. Judge E. has sent a note saying that Miss E. is (feeling) too poorly to go out. She was well enough however to go to Carreño's concert[22] at this same hour.

November 26, 1862

Received a note from Judge E. asking me to call at his house tomorrow a.m. Cannot, am going to Tarrytown.

November 27, 1862

Thanksgiving day spent at Tarrytown.

---

[22] Mr. Russel appears a bit perturbed that a young person would rather attend a concert than call up spirits with her father. But who can blame her? The concert she attended featured the Venezuelan-born, child pianist Maria Theresa Carreño, who played a selection of classical pieces. She made her stage debut on this night at the age of nine, the start of a tour through the United States.

November 29, 1862

The brother of Miss Menzies & his wife & child have come to the house to stay, pursuant to the advice of a fortune teller as Miss M. tells me. She says that Mrs. Menzies has heard the front door open and the spirit walk up stairs & that she has followed him up to the second story supposing it to be an intruder. Of course, she found nobody. On the return of Miss M., the sister-in-law insisted on a search being made for the visitor whom, as she insisted, had gone upstairs & had not come down.

Later in the evening as she was alone in the kitchen with her infant, the family were [*sic*] alarmed by a shriek - and on going down to her they found her pale and trembling. So soon as she could, she told them that as she was sitting attending to her child she heard the door behind her open & some one enter. She supposed that it was her husband but on turning round found that there was no one there.

November 30, 1862

Called on Judge Edmonds & told him of the continued trouble at 107. After berating the folly of women who are frightened because a spirit comes into the room, he promised to take his daughter to the house. Miss E. entered while we were talking. She is very pale and thin, light hair, light eyes & has not a very pleasant impression when at rest, but in conversation her face lights up beautifully. She fully sympathizes with the frightened women and made an appointment to go to the house on the 2^d Dec. She also appointed to talk with me Dec. 1 from 3 to 5 p.m.

December 1, 1862

Called on Miss Edmonds and had a talk in the library of the influences of Spiritualism upon her religious views in showing her the errors of her church - of the information it gave her in astronomy - of the uselessness of it to her in studying French - how her time was devoted to explaining her views to others and how much good was effected in reclaiming men from a low to a higher life - and of the improvement of her health under it. Her failing to keep her former appointment was owning not to the weather but to the physical condition in which she was, which rendered spiritual insight very exhausting.

She recommends great caution & great patience in investigating and that nothing be accepted until thoroughly proved. Her father's test, by which he became satisfied of his wife's presence[23] would not have satisfied her. She sees an average of seven spirits a day and has done so for eight years past - has seen none today. Told me of the test which convinced her that what she saw did not proceed from her own mind - the story of the old man who wanted her to see his wife but could not tell her where his wife was - weeks afterwards met her on the steamboat and told her that she was going to see his wife. At the Tremont House, a woman

---

[23] Judge Edmonds was very much in love with his late wife. Before he died in 1874, he asked to be buried "in the same grave with my wife, not by her side, but in the same grave, that our ashes will mingle, and be one on earth, as our souls will be one in the spirit world." His gravestone reads, "Death joins the ties, Which earth destroys."

came in when she immediately stopped and told her that she was the wife of this man, &c.

She spoke of the moral aid the spirits gave her, and how wisely they counseled her and how more wisely they withheld counsel where it was important that she should act for herself. Spoke of the happy effect it had had on her father - of the necessity of spirits communicating by inferior spirits - how her mother for a year had no communication with her save through a coarse Irishman - she says that Miss Menzies will (be) a medium for physical manifestations for a year, when they will cease & she will become a medium of impressions, that I will never be a medium exception by intuition - truth - flashing unexpectedly into the mind.

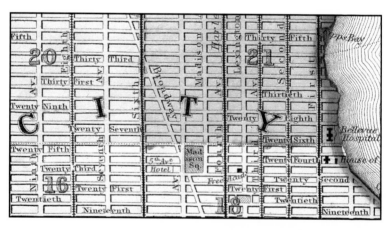

107 East 27th was between Fourth and Lexington Avenues.

Mitchell's New General Atlas, 1865

The Third Circle

December 2, 1862

While waiting for Judge E. & his daut. to arrive, I had a talk with Miss M. She described the spirit whom she saw & his dress - dark coat - a frock but not like mine - more of a sack - vest open in part sufficiently to show a great deal of his shirt bosom - not dirty - a gentleman but careless of himself.

Met Judge Edmonds and his daughter at 107 - Miss Menzies present. Miss E. commenced by conversing with Miss M. about the family experiences. She complained of the effect of the house on her - of the "terrestrial magnetism" - had never been so unpleasantly affected - her head felt as if she had been taking wine. After conversing a little while she said very quietly and naturally, "I see a spirit now - he stands there against that projection with his legs crossed - now he steps forward."

"How is he dressed?" asked I.

"Dark frock coat, vest unbuttoned - loose collar."

"Is he a gentleman?"

"No."

"Miss Menzies said the spirit she saw was gentlemanly."

"Perhaps her idea of a gentleman differs from mine. He is coarse and low but he has a tremendous will of his own. If I had such a will I should walk up and down this room with a vengeance. Yet, he has not a bad heart and has some humor."

Then she exclaimed, "Oh" and seemed impelled from the chair where she was sitting to the table where I was writing or ready to write, and seized my paper. She seemed entirely self-possessed and in her ordinary condition and said pleasantly, "If I had had any idea that he was going to take hold of me I would have prepared myself but I never was seized so violently. I asked him why he took me rudely and he says he did not know that he would affect me so violently. He has a great deal of good in him but he was low and that is why he hovers the earth.

She then seemed driven to write and to obey a rude & powerful force. She was not at her ease. The pencil was forced down upon the paper and apparently was trying to begin, but three times after succeeded only in scratching some illegible zigzag marks upon the paper. Her father remonstrated against the rudeness of the unseen agent but she told him not to interfere and after a few minutes - two or three - wrote as follows:

"My friends, [a long struggle again]

I will, as sure as there is a God in Heaven, have my way. I feel that there is a chance to do my will and if you will help me I will not hurt you but I am bound, by ties too strong yet to break, to earth and only need kindness and hope to make me free. I am sick in soul and have made up my mind to help myself. I will and must have my way and know what I am about. Silly woman, I won't hurt you but you can be a lamp to me out of darkness and I will bless you forever."

Miss Edmonds then continued playing with her pencil and talking:

"He was a very sanguine man who had a great many plans which he insisted on carrying out in his own way. He would not heed advice and he met with constant disappointments. Oh, he has had some terrible disappointment."

"What is his name?"

"He will not tell."

"What countryman is he?"

"I do not know, he will not say anything about himself."

"Has he anything to do with the Menzies family."

"No."

"Is he associated with the house?"

"No. He found this house and came here and finds it comfortable and he enjoys walking up and down in it. He finds the next state of being much better than he had any right to expect and he does not know that he can rise any higher. But if he could be engaged in some disinterested work for some person he would become more elevated and heaven would take him up – that is very rude – why do you speak to me in that manner?"

"What is that Laura?" asked the judge.

"He says he does not believe a damned word of it. That is not the only low thing he has said to me this evening."

"What else did he say?" asked her father.

"No, I will not gratify him by repeating it."

She then said that she (sensed) another spirit in the room - a young woman of a very beautiful expression, clear complexion, brown and very handsome hair about 16 years old, with white tapering fingers. Miss Menzies said that it was her sister.

Miss Edmonds then went on to say that this female spirit would always be near Miss Menzies to protect her and would prevent the man from doing any harm - that she was in no wise connected with the man but finding him in the house with Miss M. wished to use him as a means of communicating with her family and hoped through him to develop Miss M. into a medium.

Indeed the whole drift of her remarks was to reconcile Miss M. to the idea of becoming a medium of this man's communication. She then described a beautiful boy of about two years old with beautiful hair and bounding motion never taking a step but with a skip or jump - very fastidious however and fixed in his likes and ways of having things done. Miss Menzies said that this was a little boy who had lived in the house in which they had lived some two years before and who had been very much attached to her.

Miss Edmonds then said, "I see a female spirit standing near you Mr. Russel. She is of about my height with high cheek bones, the lower part of the face smaller - dark brown hair - dark eyes - a very careful affectionate expression - she wore dark clothes when living and I should suppose was very fond of Geraniums for she has a Geranium leaf in her bosom now. Do you recognize her?"

I told her that it was a very faithful description of my wife so far as it went except as to the Geraniums and about those I did not remember.

"There is an old lady standing near her - a very small old lady, in a cap and with silver white hair - features finely cut and a most benevolent expression."

I did not recognize the original.

"There is a gentleman too - tall with a small head - piercing eye - with a face wasted by disease. He was a man who knew what he was about and made sharp bargains - looked well to his interests."

I failed again to recognize the person.

"There is another female figure about you Mr. Russel - but she died a long time ago when she was about twelve years old - a very beautiful bright face."

"Are you sure she is connected with me? For I have no recollection of any such person."

"Yes she is in some way. She will come to you one of these days."

Subsequently, as she was standing up and trying to magnetize Miss Menzies, she turned to me. "Had your wife a box the color of the edge of that table [mahogany] about so long [6 inches] and so wide [4 inches] and so deep [2 inches]? I presume it holds trinkets or jewelry or something very pleasantly associated with her early days. She just showed it to me in her hand."

I replied that I remembered some half dozen boxes containing articles belonging to my wife but no box of that description. "But if she is here and sees that I do not recognize it why does she not tell you directly what it is?"

"Because I cannot now see it. It came to me when my mind was passive & flashed upon me as a daguerreotype is painted. Now that I am thinking of it I cannot receive it. But I can give you much better impressions of your wife at my own home than here where the sphere is so uncongenial."

After she had again encouraged Miss Menzies to speak to the walking visitor the next time she saw him, the session ended.

On my return home I related the account of her mother to Sophie but before speaking of the Geraniums, stopped and asked her "What flowers or plant did your mother particularly like?"

She answered, "I do not remember her particular preference for any unless it may have been Geraniums for I have a letter of yours upstairs to me when I was a little girl enclosing a Geranium leaf which you said your mother sends you."

Note by Sophie Russel: My mother died July 1844 and the only likeness of her was a daguerreotype in my father's locked wardrobe, one in my locked box and one in Boston. Not a dozen people knew of these, and no one out of her immediate family ever saw them. On examining mine with a magnifying glass I discovered a sprig of what looked like Geraniums placed in her shawl. The description is very exact.

December 5, 1862

Friday evening - called on Emma Hardinge[24] at her request for the purpose of talking over her plan for her institution. After exhausting that subject I asked her, "What do you mean by spiritualism?"

Emma Hardinge

"I mean," she replied, "the facts proving existence of unseen spirits who manifest themselves to us and communicate to us and are interested to advance us, and then the teachings of those spirits."

December 7, 1862

Sunday evening called on Miss Hardinge and had a talk with her and Mrs. Jackson on the power of prophecy. Miss H. claims this power.

---

[24] Emma Hardinge was a well-known medium and inspirational speaker.

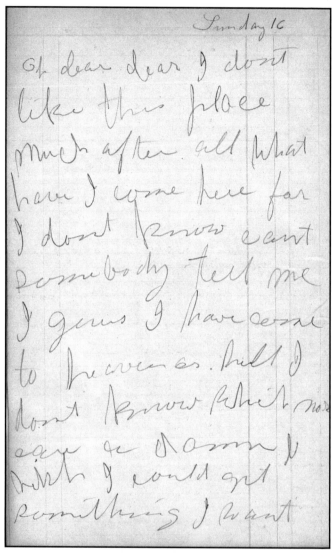

Example of Automatic Writing
Unidentified Medium, 1859
Author's Collection

Interlude

About this point in my reading of Mr. Russel's manuscript, I felt the need to learn about other aspects of this phenomenon he called "spiritualism." A man of words, I began to read from myriad printed sources about the backdrop against which these spirit circles first occurred. What I discovered was enlightening and greatly assisted my understanding of what I had been studying.

It appears that in the 19th century, a new discovery altered the manner in which living humans would think about presence of spirits. Two sisters, living in the hamlet of Hydesville in the state of New York, realized they could communicate with the spirits of those who had passed. I learned that in 1848, a young lady named Maggie Fox and her younger sister Kate discovered they could communicate with the spirit world using a most simple method. In their haunted farmhouse, spirits of the dead produced knocking or rapping sounds in response to questions posed to them by the sisters themselves or other members of their family.

Along with their older sister Leah, the gifted sisters attained instant celebrity and before long toured our young country and the European continent demonstrating their extraordinary abilities. Soon, people across the world, who seemed to have the same gift, were speaking to spirits and receiving answers through this crude form of "telegraphy."

Mediums discovered novel methods of receiving messages from the spirit world. Some of them descended into a trance state and received messages by pointing to letters and numbers printed on a board, ever so gradually spelling out words the spirit wanted the questioner to read. Others articulated messages from the spirit in an altered voice, not knowing the words he or she was uttering. Some mediums discovered spirits were capable of gaining control of their free will, forcing them to write messages from the other side. They would write unreadable letters and words, gradually forming readable sentences. Entire books have been written in this manner, the authors being ethereal and the mediums simply being their earthly tools.

I am afraid I am digressing from the topic at hand. "A little learning is a dangerous thing," Alexander Pope once wrote. So now, armed with a little learning, please continue with Mr. Russel's investigation.

New York City (Broadway) in 1862
Library of Congress

The Fourth Circle

December 9, 1862

Tuesday evening. Met at No. 107 by appointment - Miss Hardinge, Mr. & Mrs. Underhill,[25] Miss Menzies, Miss Scobell, Miss Russel.

Miss Scobell tells us she too has seen the spirit, that on Sunday p.m. as she went out into the entry her thoughts engrossed by another subject she saw a man in a dark grey dress - the colors were distinct and there was a difference between the grey of the coat and that of the pantaloons - that at first she retreated back into the sitting room but afterwards concluded to go towards him and down stairs to the family - that he vanished as she approached, and seemed to go over the banisters.

A circle was formed. Miss Hardinge expressed a feeling of oppression - suffocation by the "horrible influence" of the place. She shivered and seemed to be disgusted, almost to lose her temper - "never felt so horribly" &c.

Mrs. Underhill proposed that I should try some test experiments. I did so but they failed almost entirely. Miss Hardinge suggested that we had met for a different purpose and had no right to use the time otherwise. Mrs. Underhill then called for the spirit of Mr. Underhill's father.

---

[25] Mrs. Leah Underhill was the older sister of Margaret and Katie Fox who discovered spirit rapping. In 1858, she married Daniel Underhill and resided in New York. Upon her marriage, she decided not to sit in public circles any longer. Her presence here shows she continued her spiritual involvement in small circles.

Several solid, respectable, Quaker raps answered the summons. He was then asked to state what he saw there. Mrs. Underhill uses the alphabet verbally & says that it drives her crazy to put anything between her and the spirit. The old gentleman's answer was, "I see nothing evil but much to investigate. We will enhance your happiness and if you improve the opportunity now opening before you there will be a new and glorious future for you and yours. Levi."

Calls for the spirit were then made in vain. Mrs. Underhill proposed that we go into a perfectly dark room in the hope that he there would manifest himself. We accordingly went upstairs into a room as dark as a room with closed blinds without curtains or shutters usually is. It was dark enough for any reasonable spirit. With my back to the windows I could see nothing whatsoever.

A circle was formed by taking hands and the most affectionate appeals to the invisible tenant were made to no purpose. Miss Menzies says that he was in the room for a few moments passing behind me and going through the door into the adjoining room. In vain were arguments addressed and efforts made to show him. How much we wanted to help him. He gave no sign. Invitations were then given to other spirits and raps came in great number.

These raps usually came upon the floor but on request struck the door against which one of us was standing so that the vibration was distinct. They were all, however, in the neighborhood of Mrs. Underhill and could not be obtained at any spot distant from her. They were very significant and each had a peculiar property character, though the persons called for were unknown.

"Is Frank here?"

A hard clear rap.

"Is Sarah here?"

A gentle familiar rap.

"Is Willie here?"[26]

A tiny child's knock on the floor.

"Is Neddy here?"[27]

The same as Willie's

No explanation was given leading any of the company to know, beforehand, who the persons called for were, nor was there any change in my voice in passing from Lucy to Willie and Neddie.   Abandoning all hope of hearing from our particular spirit tonight we returned to the room where we had met. When I called for Sarah and three quiet unobtrusive raps answered.   I then asked for such a message as would satisfy me of her presence. The response was:

"I will watch over you and manifest myself alone to you when I can and make you happy."

I replied, "Sarah you know me very well and you know that such a message as that will never satisfy me," but I received nothing more in return.

I then called for Frank and think I asked him to tell me something I did not know before.   But all the answer I received was, "I will go with you tomorrow night." I had an appointment to met Miss Hardinge and the Managers of her Institution the next evening at Mrs. Underhill's.

---

[26] Deceased son of William and Sarah Russel.
[27] Another deceased son of William and Sarah; Mr. Russel spelled his name two different ways in his journal.

December 10, 1862

Leah Fox Underhill

Wednesday evening met with the Managers of the Woman's Industrial Farm at Mrs. Underhill's. After discussing Miss Hardinge's plans, the others left and I remained with Mr. & Mrs. Underhill, Miss Hardinge and Mr. Britton.[28] It was 11 o'clock and I had pretty much given up the idea of spiritual manifestations for that night. But I silently called for Frank several times. I received no reply.

At length, I took a seat near Mrs. Underhill & reminded her of my brother's promise made the night before. "Yes," said she, "I have been thinking of it & wondering why he does not come."

We called for him distinctly. There was no immediate answer but after a few minutes, loud sharp raps were heard on the floor. Mrs. Underhill then proceeded to show that her contact either directly or through another medium was necessary to produce the raps. She threw the door open and touching it with the tip of her finger asked that the raps might be given on that door. They were so given and so powerfully that the door vibrated in my hand. She repeated the experiment & told me to hold my ear to the door. I did so and the raps came smart and heavy on the other side of the

---

[28] This refers to Mr. William Britten, Miss Hardinge's future husband whom she married in 1870.

door. I then put my ear on the sound side and the sounds came from the first. The vibration of the wood in my hand was not to be mistaken.

Mrs. Underhill then stood a foot from the door and I asked the raps to strike the door - but they did not. She put her finger within an inch of the wood but with the same result. She then touched the corner of her silk apron to the wood and the raps struck the door clear as hammer strokes.

In the course of conversation, Mrs. U. said that Major Rains of the Rebel Army was one of the most candid investigators. To this, "Frank" expressed his assent by three hearty raps - and being interrogated by me said that it was he, Frank, who rapped and that he meant to say that this rebel Major, who placed torpedoes in the way of our troops, <u>was</u> one of the most candid investigators. [29]

---

[29] Major Gabriel James Rains resigned from the U.S. Army in 1861 to join the Confederacy. Although 'Frank' is implying that Rains had died, Rains lived beyond the end of the war.

December 13, 1862

During the night of the 11th and 12th, Miss Menzies and her mother heard the noise of a fearful contest in the room overhead - men struggling, scuffling, wrestling and finally a body falling to the ground with a force that shook house, and as it fell dragging furniture down with it. The time seems to be after midnight. The old lady is excessively terrified and hears what she never heard before (she says she is somewhat deaf) the sounds of steps hurrying down stairs. The same noise is heard again on the night of the 12th and 13th. The women are awaked from sleep by it and do not know the hour but say that it is well into the night.

On the evening of the 12th, as the family were at tea, loud raps were heard upon the floor overhead. On rushing up to the old lady who is alone in her room, they are told that she knows nothing of the noise, neither made it nor heard it. On the evening of the 13th at tea time, the same raps are heard in the kitchen.

December 14, 1862

Called at No. 107 and talked an hour with Miss M. combatting [*sic*] her objections to communicating with the spirit. He has annoyed her by getting under her bed and raising her up, by pulling the bedclothes down even when she places them under her head in order to prevent it, and by his generally disagreeable ways that he has an almost incongruable [*sic*] repugnance to any communication to or from her.

I tell her that Mrs. Underhill was so tossed from her bed that finally she had to sleep on the floor, and that Laura Edmonds had her bedclothes pulled off night after night and endured every variety of annoyance for a year because she would not yield to the desire of the spirits to communicate through her, and I argue that the object is the same in this case and that the result will be the same.

December 16, 1862

Tuesday. Miss Scobell tells S.[30] that last evg., as she was lighting the gas in the hall, the light fell directly upon the spirit standing near her. She immediately retreated into the bedroom and locked the door. After he has disappeared she cannot recall his head at all - when she looks at him she does not miss anything but afterward she cannot remember that she saw his head - the dress is distinctly impressed on her mind.

---

[30] Referring to Russel's daughter Sophie.

December 17, 1862

Miss Menzies says that last night the spirit walked about their room tapping various articles of furniture and afterwards scratching them as if with his finger nail. She says that her little nephew, three years old, hears the footsteps and retreats from them to her, slips down from table if he is seated on the side toward them, and cannot be induced to return. She cannot make up her mind to speak to him. She says that it is not within her volition, that she is paralyzed by his presence.

December 18, 1862

Thursday. Conversazione[31] at Mrs. Underhill's. Present some sixty persons, among them Greeley,[32] Manning and wife, H. P. Townsend, Calhoun and wife.

Miss Hardinge addressed the company in what was said to be a state of trance and announced Mrs. U's intention to hold these meetings periodically for the purposes of scientific investigation. She then offered to speak on any topic which might be proposed. The following questions were then asked & answered substantially thus:

Qn. In which condition do spirits find themselves immediately after leaving the flesh?

---

[31] A conversational gathering usually to discuss art, science, or literature. In this case, they discussed spiritualistic matters.

[32] An apparent reference to Horace Greeley, editor of the *New York Tribune*. He became involved in American spiritualism and was a serious investigator of the subject.

Ans.   We are spirits here, we shall be the same spirits there. We shall have relinquished these bodies but we shall have similar aspirations there and here.

Qn.   Any additional faculty given there?

Ans.   Tis the sixth sense or sense of intuition or immediate apprehension of knowledge.

Qn.   What is the object of spiritual manifestations?

Ans.   To attract attention and open the way to communication.

Qn.   Is the touch of my child's hand substantial?

Ans.   The spirits use Electricity Galvanism[33] or any subtle agent in Nature to produce the effect they wish. In this way the thing that touches your hand is substance.

Qn.   Are spirits attracted to a locality or dissipated through all space?

Ans.   As Napoleon's mind did not need more room than did the mind of an ordinary man so the spirit on the other side does not need space any more than it did here. It is individualized & therefore cannot be lost or dissipated. But it may (be) attracted and attached to partial & local affairs in this world.

Qn.   How are spirits to be identified?

Ans.   Only by increasing the moral power of the investigator can doubt as to identity be removed.

---

[33] Use of direct electrical current to stimulate or heal.

December 19, 1862

Miss Hardinge calls at my office with a letter from James M. Gale of Eugene City, Oregon, on behalf of Hillyard Shaw of the same place, stating that the testator, under the advice of the late Dr. Robert Hare[34] in the spirit, had bequeathed to her all his estate to be applied to the purposes of the Woman's Industrial Farm. She expects to yield from $5000 to $7000.

She has asked Jackson Davis[35] to visit No. 107.

Miss Menzies tells me that the wrestling & scuffling and falling were repeated last night at 107 - and that the body came to the floor with a force compared with which the falling of the back of the chimney in the same room a few weeks ago was nothing.

---

[34] Robert Hare, M. D. was a highly respected Professor Emeritus of chemistry at the University of Pennsylvania. He began to investigate spiritualism believing it to be delusional. His experiments proved to him otherwise and he himself later became a medium. He had professional relationships with both Henry Gordon and Judge Edmonds. Hare died in 1858 and was kind enough to communicate with Hillyard Shaw from the other side and encourage him to leave his estate to Miss Hardinge's cause.

[35] Andrew Jackson Davis was a popular spiritualist who became famous as the "Poughkeepsie Seer" as a young man. He wrote numerous books on the subject of spiritualism, some of which were dictated to him from the spirit world.

December 20, 1862

Call at No. 107 wither Mr. Washington had repaired in order to watch for the spirit & having detected him suddenly to jump in on him. Had a talk with Miss Scobell.

The scuffling was renewed last night, though with less violence than in the preceding night.

Miss S. says that when she goes upstairs frightened and trembling and believing that something dreadful is to happen, nothing troubles her. But that whenever she makes up her mind to be courageous & meet whatever may occur, the spirits trouble her more than ever, running upstairs behind her, making noises in the closets.

December 21, 1862

Heard part of Jackson Davis' lecture on Hospitals and Charity. Good but trite. Saw an excellent spiritual photograph, the property of a brother from Norwalk Conn. Davis is engaged for this p.m. and cannot attend at No. 107. Miss Hardinge will meet me there with a medium tomorrow.

The Fifth Circle

December 22, 1862

Monday. At 107 met Miss Hardinge, Mrs. Jackson, Mr. Hardinge, David Felt, Miss Menzies & Miss Scobell. Mrs. Adie Boucher had been invited but had declined because her husband was not included. Miss H. had sent a note of explanation including Mr. B. in the programme. As they did not appear, Miss H. & I went after them & brought them. Mrs. Jackson had talked with her before but we did not & she professed not to know the story of the house - said that she had merely heard that it was haunted.

Soon after coming into the room she professed to be very unpleasantly affected by the influence of the house - shuddered and looked towards the recess and seemed to be chilled from that direction - but the door was tight & window ditto.

At 9:15, the circle was formed around the table and sat at first in silence with clasped hands. Mrs. Boucher shivers - complains of a choking influence - had the same at home this evening after receiving Miss H's note when she felt this same influence as if some one was drowning her. After a quarter of an hour, hands are unclasped & we convened. Mrs B. had been silent & absorbed in her own consciousness now writes:

Spirit: "I am with you - who wants to see or know me?"

Omnes: "I do" - "So do I" - "We all do."

Spirit: Writes "I will not harm you."

Russel: "You have told us that five & twenty times."

Spirit: Writes "I am not alone."

Felt: "Will he tell his name - who is he?"

Spirit: Writes "There are two of us here. Keep quiet."

Mrs. B: "There are two distinct influences one better than the other, one more mild the other more gross, then there comes another more gentle."

9:45: A long pause and silence.

Mrs. B: "I see two forms but I don't know why they don't show themselves more distinctly. It seems as if they hated to show themselves.

Russel: "Where are they?"

Mrs. B: "Between you [Felt] and her [Miss Menzies]."

(At Mrs. B's request the gas is put down. She says the gas light destroys this light.)

A long pause in silence ensued.

(Mrs. B. seems to labor, sighs. Miss M. says that the spirit has been here two or three times, a few minutes each time.)

Mrs. B: "One of these spirits is a man, gross heavy built, rather tall, dark appearance, a peculiar eye, keen penetrating, but such frowns! He frowns, he don't like to be described at all. Is awful mad. Does not seem to care much, does not seem to want to be known, he is callous in his appearance.

Russel: "How is he dressed?"

Mrs. B: "He wears a coat in cloak-style, heavy with a half cape in front, not exactly that, but the sleeves seem to be large - dark color - dark grey between a gray and a black. The coat is drawn together - now he throws his cloak back."

Russel: "Is he a gentleman?"

Mrs. B: "He has not really the appearance of a gentleman. He seems to be dreadfully out about something. [To Mrs. Jackson] Were you talking to him?"

Mrs. Jackson: "No, I was wishing him well."

Mrs. B: "He was answering you. I don't like his influence at all. There is another influence here. I am very glad of it."

(She points over her shoulder to the back of the room under the recess.)

Mrs. B: "He is a fighting character - can tell by his looks. It's back there anyway - his head was hurt. There is a female around here also. [Starts] Somebody put a hand on me - mild, but there is something not right about her connected with him some way or other. When he died he died violently - struggled hard for his life. There seems to be a wound on his temple, about his neck too - puts his hand to his heart - has been hurt there. Oh there is an awful influence here tonight [feels her throat]. Oh Lord! [feels her throat again and seems to suffer] His throat is cut. Oh! I don't want to see it - it sickens me - the sight of them. [She feels for him] He is not old - this man was fond of drink."

Russel: "Will he say where he was buried?"

Mrs. B: "I think this man was buried twice - Back there - the whole thing was" [points towards the recess]

Russel: "Do you mean in the back of the lot or the back of the room."

Mrs. B: "Well back there the whole thing was. It seems to have been only for a short time. He shows me a large body of water. I think he was finally drowned but back there he was buried. I think this occurred considerable time ago."

Russel: "Why does he want to come back?"

Spirit: Writes "Because I wish to show that dead men tell tales sometimes - money - a woman was the cause somewhat."

Mrs. B: "He feels very kindly towards you." [Miss M]

Spirit: Writes "You need not fear and I will not harm you."

Felt: "He will tell when this happened."

Spirit: Writes "This time of the day and year."

Mrs. B: "I don't think he was really a bad man at heart. He looks as if he were a person who had travelled a good deal. He is considerable dark. I think he was a foreigner - looks like a Spanish descent. He says we will hear a noise. What do you wish us to do?"

Spirit: Writes "I have not come to that yet - the woman you see was the man's <u>wife</u>."

Mrs. B: "Spirit will you explain what you mean. Whose wife? He says she is the wife of the man that killed him."

(We then talked about Miss Menzies communicating with him.)

Mrs. B: Writes "I wish no harm to them but to free my spirit from the chains which hold me. I could not progress till this - You may think me cruel but forgive me. I will not trouble them disagreeably."

(Conversation about his going home with different ones of the company.)

Mrs. B: Writes "I shall go where I feel that I am received."

Mrs. B: "He had faculties which were capable of being developed very usefully."

Felt: "Will he give us his name?"

Mrs. B: Writes "I am not ready to go yet."

Felt: "Can you show yourself to us all?"

(Mrs. B. raps three times with her fingers.)

Mrs. B: Writes "Put the light down."

Here Miss Menzies and Miss Scobell became terrified and rushed from the circle which was accordingly broken up. The conversation that followed was desultory. Mrs. B. writes, "You think me more vile than I was." She then asked him to rap three times distinctly but obtained no reply. On being pushed for his name he wrote through Mrs. B., "H" - "Goodbye for now."

As the company began to disperse, Miss Hardinge, in a trance state, addressed Miss Menzies and Miss Scobell. She denied that any blood had been shed in that house but said that the walls were charged with the bad influences of bad deeds committed there and violent passions indulged there. She advised against investigations of this kind but directed them to search for the pure & peaceful.

Note by Mr. Russel: While the proceedings were going on, Miss Hardinge wrote, "There is a woman here, a coarse low woman who seems to me to look in at that window. She wears a cap and her hair is about her face." There is a peculiar combination of influences here.

December 23, 1862

Miss Menzies says that the steps were heard all night pacing the room above, coming down stairs and into her room, going up again, and going through the same performance without an intermission of five minutes, one incessant walking.

Tuesday ev'g. Spent an hour with old Mrs. Menzies and Miss Scobell. The old lady has now heard the steps - says that she probably does not hear as readily as others. But she heard the wrestling overhead. Just over her bed and apparently in the recess, and the same night she heard the steps coming down stairs. She believes it to be spiritual and suggests old Gantion again.

She says that on the occasion of the wrestling the house shook as the body fell. She tells me that her daughter in law, Donald's wife, saw a figure in white in the kitchen on one of the past evenings after coming there.

December 24, 1862

Miss Menzies tells me that her sister-in-law had that morning told her that Donald, the night before, woke up, heard a noise in the room as if someone creeping. He turned and saw the figure of a man. He sat up in his bed, rubbed his eyes and looked at him steadily. The figure made signs as if to draw attention to a Spanish cloak he wore. Then Menzies recognized him as a man named Antoine, whom twelve years ago he had known in South America and who left there on account of politics with about $5000. Donald tried to speak to him but could not and after a little time the figure went away. Miss M. says that last night the figure knocked at the bedroom door before entering.

December 25, 1862

Miss Menzies says that she heard the steps last night but that they were comparatively quiet. They came into the room without knocking.

December 26, 1862

Friday p.m. Went over to 107 to enquire about the old lady and found that she was very low. Saw Miss M. She says that the spirit was in the room last night but was quiet - made no disturbance. Had an interview with Donald.

Donald is a carpenter, 39 years old, light hair, eyes and complexion. Occasionally drinks too much - did so yesterday but now he seemed all right. He says they came to 107 Nov. 25, that two or three days after coming, his wife began to talk to him about strange noises. He never heard any thing until last week at tea table when knocks came as if in the hall. He went up to see if his mother wanted any thing. Before that he had heard noises but had attributed them to rats. He had not heard about the investigations there at the time the following occurred:

A week ago last Monday [he was very particular about the time and when I cross examined him as to it (he) stuck to his first statement], he was lying in bed awake and happening to turn saw a figure standing in the room about ten feet from the bed. The room was pitch dark but there was sufficient light about the figure. He had a Spanish wrapper. [they are worn by passing the head through a hole in the middle and letting the rest fall down towards the feet]. He wore no hat - had jet black hair - light eyes - light complexion for a Spaniard - about 32 years old. He was standing still looking at me. Was quite pleasant - it did not seem as if any thing disturbed him - tried to speak to him but could not - looked at one another two or three minutes - I was lying down when he disappeared. Donald remained awake & after the disappearance awoke his wife & asked her if she had seen any thing. She said no but that she had a cold dread over her as if there was something troubling her in her sleep.

He recognized the figure as that of Antonio - whom he knew at Tobago, 13 miles from Panama. He was a Chilian by birth & from Valparaiso - a single man - not in any one's permanent employment. In 1848, he and Donald together took the job of repairing the house of Padre Angola. In 1848, he started for Peru - he had been charged with having been engaged in piracy on the coast and had to leave with about $100. That is all Donald knew of, though it was reported that Antonio had more. He had an accomplice named Ponce who gave heavy bail at Panama. He did not tell the rest of the family of this vision until after he had heard of the occurences in the house.

<u>N. B.</u> He knew of all the occurrences in the house Dec. 21. When Miss Menzies related them to him and his wife. That after this apparition he began to notice the raps - they were those heard at the tea table as already spoken of.

<u>Note from Mr. Russell</u>: It will appear from the statement of his wife that the apparition was subsequent to these raps.

Christmas night he saw the figure again. He was lying awake, turned over and was attracted by something - looked out into the room and there was the same figure in the same dress as before and nearly in the same place - had the same appearance as before. Looked at one another two or three minutes when it disappeared. Did not do any thing, had no power to do so - wanted to but could not. After the disappearance, woke his wife and asked if she had seen anything and she said no but that she had a cold dread as something were happening in her sleep. Has not the least doubt of its being Antonio. Nelson[36] was our consul at Panama in Nov. 1848.

I then saw Donald's wife. She says that the date of the first apparition was last Monday Dec. 22 and not a week previously, that it was approaching morning and she was awake and her husband asked her if she did not see any thing - but she did not - that the second vision was manifest about 11 o'clock Christmas night - she saw that Donald was absorbed and he asked her if she had not seen any thing but she had not. She did feel a chill as if something passing near her - that on the first evening of her coming to the house she saw a figure of whitish smoky consistency walk between her bed and the window - was not frightened but watched it till she fell asleep. That on one occasion she heard the front door open and heard steps in the hall and looked from the bedroom door to see who it was - that the steps went as far as the bottom of the stairs and ceased. She did herself go up the stairs to look for the intruder but sent her husband & Miss Menzies.

That on another occasion she heard some one rattle a stick across each of the banisters - that Dec. 14th paper seemed to be thrown against the glass partition door and Dec 24 and 25 water seemed to be dashed against it. That on this last occasion her baby heard it. She denies that she was so much frightened by the opening & shutting of a door and apparent entrance of steps as to shriek on the occasion alluded to; she says she only called her husband.

---

36 William Nelson was U.S. Consul in Panama City from 1841-1849.

December 27, 1862

Robert Dale Owen[37] called on me today. I proposed that he should make a fresh investigation without informing himself of the previous stories or experiments, taking with him a medium who knew no more about them than himself. I told him merely who occupied the house & that the health of the occupants suffered from the disturbance and that there had been a degree of unanimity in the former experiments. Gave him a letter to Miss M. asking her to let him visit the house.

December 28, 1862

Called on R.D. Owen - Conversation on apparitions. Gave me his book. Is to take Foster[38] to the house - has been there himself & talked with Miss M. who told him she had seen a spirit.

January 2, 1863

Last evening Miss Scobell told me that the walking had continued since I was last there. She has seen a new spirit two or three times, his back - dress black, tight fitting coat - black hair parted in the middle behind - no hat.

---

[37] Robert Dale Owen was former Chargé d'Affaires and later Minister at Naples. Following in his father's footsteps, he became a spiritualist, vowing not to rest until he proved whether survival of the personality after death was a reality.

[38] This fleeting reference may refer to Charles H. Foster, an American medium of questionable repute.

January 16, 1863

Donald Menzies has just left me. He says that he has twice heard water dashed against the partition, and noises as if of breaking the glass. One night this week, as he was falling to sleep, a ball seemed to fall on his temple and run down his body as far as his knees where it stopped. He pushed it off and it fell with a heavy sound on the floor. But nothing was to be found.

Old Mrs. Menzies died on the 5th.[39]

Last evening attended a party at Mrs. Underhill's. Present Mrs. Hardinge, Dr. & Mrs. Hallock, Robert Dale Owen, Oliver Johnson, H. P. Townsend, Mr. & Mrs. Calhoun and some fifty others. Miss Hardinge read a communication from Red Jacket[40] upon our political prospects - in which he spoke of the treacheries we are to undergo under the name of peace - also some other communications. She went into a trance state and discoursed of prophecy. This, she says, is not the result of the judgment deducing the future from the past but intuition. She spoke of the "infinite now" of God to whom there is no past no future.

Dr. Hallock said that the purpose of spiritual manifestations is to teach that the violation of the moral law is as certainly to be followed by punishment as the violation of a physical law is. The weather was damp and foggy and the raps were faint.

---

[39] Her funeral was held at 10 o'clock on Wednesday January 7th from her home at 107 E. 27th Street.
[40] The Native American Red Jacket was a popular spirit to call upon. He was known as a great orator.

The Sixth Circle

January 19th, 1863

On the 19th a circle was formed in Miss M's room consisting of Dr. & Mrs. Neal, Dr. & Mrs. Perly, and Dr. Stotz.

Mrs. Neal was the medium. At first she (had) a severe pain in the right temple, faint & sick and almost paralyzed by pain in her limbs as if by bruises. She said that for 24 hours previously her speech had been taken from her until about an hour before the meeting. She seemed to be affected very much as Mrs. Boucher had been.

She asked, "Has this spirit ever appeared to any one in a bruised & mutilated condition?" She said "He has appeared to me in that state" and she seemed sick from the sight. She said there was hardly a bone in his body but it was bruised - that his arm was broken. She stopped a little while - all this time the spirit had been standing between Miss M. & Mrs. Neal but rather behind Miss M. so that she did not see him.

During this pause, Miss M. felt her chair pushed & herself shoved off & that she was compelled to go to the other end of the room. As she did so every one shivered & complained of cold on their backs. As Miss M. took her seat the spirit was behind her back. Then Mrs. Neal said: "Oh now I see him in his natural state without any bruises. He looks very differently." To this the spirit remarked, "Why do you look at me so, you must think me very handsome." This was audible to Miss M. & Mrs. Neal but not to all. This was the first time Miss Menzies had heard him speak more than a few words. The accent was slightly foreign. A conversation then ensued between him and Mrs. Neal. He told them that he did not want them there, that they need not stare at him like a pack of fools.

One gentleman said, "I speak Spanish, will you converse with me?"

The spirit answered, "If you talk like a sensible man."

The spirit was asked why he intruded on the Menzies. He replied that he had not done so, that he was there first and they had intruded on him, that he had made the others move out, and would make them move out unless.

Miss M: "You are very unjust - you know it is our poverty & not our will keeps us here, and it is wicked and cruel for you to treat us thus. Cannot we enter into an armistice? What do you mean by "unless?"

Spirit: "Unless you speak to me."

Miss M: "Well I will speak to you now."

Spirit: "That is not what I want."

Miss M: "What do you want?"

Spirit: "To see you alone with no one present, day or evening at any hour. You will appoint an hour every day or evening."

Miss M: "I give you from 11-12 in the morning when I am here. But I am not here all the time."

Spirit: "When you are not here I will follow you or appoint another hour."

During the evening a gentleman said, "I don't think your friend the spirit is here Mrs. Neal" and before she could reply Miss Menzies saw the spirit glide around from behind her chair towards the gentleman who immediately exclaimed, "Oh - I take my words back." And said the spirit had struck him in the side.

January 20, 1863

Miss Menzies says she met him the next day. He came punctually at 11 and she rec'd him alone. On this occasion he pledged her to secrecy, and to obedience to his wishes and to endeavors to do what she could for him.

He wishes a chapter of the Bible read every day before he says any thing. She has kept her appointments with him ever since. She has asked him his name. His reply was, "when I get ready I will tell you" and he has never told her. He is a Spaniard from Central America. He has twice worn a Spanish wrapper like that described by Donald Menzies - Never worn a hat - Jet black hair - Eyes which at one time seem black as a sloe's - at another they seem grey - at another brown - about 35 years of age. Dark complexion rather sallow - it may be fair for a Spaniard.

Miss Menzies is sure that it is the same person Donald saw but thinks that Donald is mistaken as to his being Antonio whom he knew at Tobago.

January 23, 1863

Miss Hardinge and Mrs. Jackson called and requested permission to bring Mr. Anderson,[41] a portrait painter of spirits. In the evening they came - Mr. & Mrs. Anderson, Mrs. Hardinge & Mrs. Jackson. After some conversation they all complained that they felt an extraordinary influence and Mrs. Anderson asked them to be still.

Miss Menzies saw the spirit standing behind Mrs. Anderson's chair. He said he did not wish to be seen but to talk with Mrs. A.

Mrs. A: "Won't you let my husband see you?"

Spirit: "Not now."

He said he would like Mr. Anderson to take his likeness. He asked Anderson to go up stairs. Anderson says he went up & offered to meet any spirit and offered his hand.

He (the spirit) told Mrs. A that he was a Spanish trader, came from Central America to the United States and that he was murdered in that house for his money, that he had a considerable sum of money about him when he came there - that he was murdered in the recess of the room on the second story.

---

[41] This appears to be Mr. W. P. Anderson, noted spirit artist from New York City.

January 24, 1863

Mr. Anderson came to the house to take the portrait. But the spirit told him that the atmosphere was so moist and the conditions were such that he could not command himself long enough to have his likeness taken, that he must come on a clear day.

January 25, 1863

Mr. Anderson came and went up stairs with a blank piece of paper and pencil. He was there alone about five minutes when he called to Miss Menzies. She went up and Anderson said that he had not called on his own account but that the spirit wanted to know if she was satisfied with that likeness. Mr. A. then showed her a perfect outline of a likeness of the spirit.[42] Miss. M. told him that it could not be more perfect. Miss M. then left. Mr. A. then remained about five minutes longer and then came down stairs leaving the picture behind.

---

[42] Unfortunately, Mr. Anderson's sketch of the spirit does not accompany Mr. Russel's manuscript.

THE HAUNTING ON EAST 27TH

Postscript

Thus ends Mr. Russel's story. Perhaps you feel as do I — a bit unsettled, desirous of further enlightenment, and filled with unrequited hope for further knowledge of the aftermath of these events; closure, if you will; a finality. These are natural human desires, but I am afraid anything else once known regarding this peculiar case has forever been lost to history. Regrettably, there are many more questions than answers...though, more hope for believers...and alas, more uncertainty for those of us who still search for truth.

I have often wondered about our Mr. Russel. Did he unearth the answers he sought? Did he become a believer in the continuance of life and consciousness on the other side? Did he find personal peace by communing with his late wife? Or, did he simply become more bewildered and mystified by the attempt? It was, perhaps, the devastating loss of Sarah that drove him to try to understand things spiritual, attempt to create order out of chaos, endeavor to transform opacity into transparency, and to try to know the unknowable. He too sought closure. I hope, for the sake of all of us who seek truth, he found that which he so painstakingly sought.

My wonderment about the nature of this man, his motives for pursuing unworldly matters, and what happened to him after his spiritual examinations inspired me to embark on some historical detective work. With only a few clues at hand, I attempted to learn more about this curious gentleman.

William Channing Russel
Faculty Biographical Files
Division of Rare and Manuscript Collections
Cornell University Library

Historical Ghost Hunting

Who was this man Russel? An informative, albeit brief, citation in a directory of the city of New York indicated only that he was a practicing lawyer. Such a common name "Russel," yet spelled in a most uncommon manner. I knew extraordinarily little about this man. I had learned where he dwelled, his occupation, the names of some of those with whom he associated, and the identities of his late wife Sarah and daughter Sophie...not a lot on which to proceed but enough, so I thought, to track down this intriguing gentleman of yesteryear.

Using all the resources at my disposal, a spirited determination, and an instinct for following paths wherever they may lead, I set about piecing together the life of this mysterious fellow. Many such investigations follow the same pattern – whereby at first, one doesn't know where to start looking. As isolated clues start to fit together and form a pattern, the inquiry becomes a bit easier – and this investigation followed a similar sequence.

One reference I fortuitously stumbled upon mentioned a William Channing Russel. This gentleman, it turns out, had given up his law practice after the death of his son in 1863 and eventually was to join the original faculty at Cornell University when it opened in 1868. Correspondence with that august institution's keeper of archives proved most beneficial.

Because of Russel's lengthy affiliation there, Cornell maintains a rather extensive collection of his personal papers. Upon scrutiny of this professor's penmanship on his personal correspondence, there could be no doubt that this was the same gentleman who, in the exact same script, wrote of his investigation into the mysterious events at 107 East 27th Street.

One clue quickly led to another and within a remarkably brief time I had found papers and publications by or about William C. Russel, Esq. in the dusty archives and book shelves at the universities of Antioch, Brown, Columbia, Cornell, Duke, Harvard, Rochester and Yale.

William Russel's story started in Boston on February 23, 1814 when he was born into the family of William W. and Lucy Russel. The Russel family moved to Sunswick (now Astoria), New York and later to that island of commerce known as Manhattan.

As a young man, Russel matriculated at Columbia College and completed his A.B. degree[43] in 1832. It was most unfortunate that the graduation for the 28 seniors was cancelled that year because of a raging yellow fever epidemic. Each graduate had prepared for the occasion by composing a commencement oration to be delivered at the graduation ceremony. Russel's eloquent address quietly rests, forever unspoken, amongst his other papers in the Carl A. Kroch Library at Cornell University.

"The Connection between Man's Knowledge and his Happiness," expressed Russel's views of the continuing improvement of man from life through eternity – achieved through knowledge. It reads in part:

---

[43] *Artium Baccalaureus* degree, nowadays more commonly called Bachelor of Arts.

"…Who would be willing to take immortality if his powers of enjoying happiness were to be no greater than they are now? It is the consciousness that we are made for constant, never ending improvement that gives its full value to man's rank in creation. Eternal improvement! Man, think of what you are and what you may become…

The mind which God has given you is the noblest gift because it is that which constitutes our resemblance to him, will you despise it? The prize offered for its improvement is continued approach to the divinity, do you not value it? The consequence of its neglect is his severest displeasure and our alienation, do you not fear it?

Onward then in the pursuit of knowledge – gain a treasure, invaluable, indestructible, enshrined in the immortality of that soul which is improved by its attainment."

Upon his departure from Columbia, Russel pursued the study of law at Harvard, graduating in 1834. Pursuing his quest of "eternal improvement," this "doublestoried" man returned to Columbia for his A.M. degree,[44] which he earned in 1835.

During the early 1830s, William Russel married Sarah Cabot Jackson, a member of quite a well-to-do family from Boston. Sarah, whom he loved dearly, bore several of his children. Willie and Neddie died in childhood (as you will recall, he attempted to communicate with them during the fourth spirit circle); they were followed by Lucy, Sophie and

---

[44] *Artium Magister*, nowadays more commonly called Master of Arts.

Cabot Jackson. Although the exact circumstances are lost to history, Sarah Jackson Russel died in July of 1844. Her death left Russel suffering with considerable grief.

It appears to have taken many years for Russel to again seek happiness and the comfort of a loving woman. On December 8, 1853, Russel married Matilda Howland, sister of Cornelia Howland (who first related the story of the haunting). They too had several children, naming their first daughter - Sarah Jackson Russel - after William's long-departed love.

Relatively little has emerged about Russel's life as a lawyer in New York, though in December, 1854 he is found attempting to sell the city of New York a Fire Alarm Telegraph, a new and significant invention of Dr. William F. Channing and Moses G. Farmer. This life-and-property-saving system had already been adopted in Boston. New York City purchased the system and it became the standard means of reporting fires. Russel sold the rights to John Nelson Gamewell and it was he who eventually introduced the system across the country.

Fortunately, Russel's earlier and later life is substantially better documented than his years in the legal profession and provides considerable insight into the man.

Personal Tragedy

Shortly after William Russel's investigation into the haunting on East 27th Street, the Civil War became very personal for his family. William and Sarah Russel's son, Cabot Jackson Russel, was attending Harvard University when he decided to join the Union Army. William Russel noted in a letter to Sophie, "An entire change has come over Cabot's prospects. It seems that he has been all along very anxious to go to the war and now is very urgent

Cabot J. Russel
Luis F. Emilio's
A Brave Black Regiment

with me to let him go. I have not yet made up my mind but suppose I should consent."[45]

Cabot joined the Massachusetts 44th Regiment and served in North Carolina for several months before being offered a promotion to Captain of the 54th Massachusetts Infantry Regiment – Company H. The 54th had recently been formed by Robert Gould Shaw of Boston and was comprised of "colored" troops. The men trained at the Readville Camp about ten miles southwest of Boston and Company H was mustered into service in May 1863. On May 28th, the men of the 54th paraded through the streets of Boston to the docks where they departed amidst cheering crowds for South Carolina via the steamer *De Molay*.

---

[45] WCR to Sophie, August 27, 1862 (Duke University)

Cabot's grandparents wanted to purchase a sword for their newly promoted grandson and they asked William to acquire it for them. William Russel's mother reminded him of his responsibility in a letter:

> "Your father says that you must buy the sword for Cabot, for that he knows nothing about such articles and if you are equally ignorant he advises you take some one with you who is more experienced to assist you in the selection. Why have you not attended to this sooner – **I** never leave things to the last moment. He will pay you when he sees you." In the same letter, she wrote of her concern, "I don't like the idea of Cabot being made Captain. He is too young & inexperienced for such a responsible position, but I suppose I am an old Fogey."[46]

On July 8th, the regiment received orders to join other regiments in an assault on the islands that guarded the entrance to Charleston's harbor. They engaged the enemy in heavy fighting on James Island before moving toward the strategically important objective of Fort Wagner on Morris Island. Fort Wagner was heavily fortified with earthworks, armaments, and 1,700 men. It was described as "the strongest single earthwork known in the history of warfare."[47]

On the 10th, the portion of the island south of the fort had been taken by Union troops and they prepared for the assault on the fort itself. When Mr. Russel first became aware of the fighting on Morris Island, he wrote to his daughter

---

[46] Mother to WCR, April 29, 1863, William C. Russel Papers, Cornell University.
[47] Emilio, 70.

Sophie, "You are mistaken as to the place attacked by our forces. It was near Charleston not 'Charlestown'. I feel anxious about the result. Mr. Shaw tells me that he heard today that Fort Wagner has been taken. But it seems to me very probable that the black regiments would be thrown forward as a forlorn hope and of course would be much cut up."[48] Russel too was mistaken; Fort Wagner had not been taken, nor would it ever be taken.

At twilight on the 18th Robert Gould Shaw's 54th Massachusetts regiment led the assault on Fort Wagner. Shaw himself was killed on the crest of the parapet and more than half his troops involved in the assault were killed, wounded or missing (many presumed killed). The fate of Captain Russel was unknown after the battle and became the subject of much investigation and speculation. A few days after the battle, William Russel received a letter[49] from F. L. Higginson, First Lieutenant of Company I from Morris Island:

> Dear Mr. Russel,
>
> I am sorry that it falls to my lot to write you about our recent fight & to tell you that nothing has been heard of Cabot since the fight. One of the sergeants told me that he was close to him & Capt. Simpkins when Cabot fell shot. Capt. S. called to him to help lift Cabot up & had no sooner done so than he fell himself directly across Cabot & never spoke afterwards. He said that C. spoke to him & seemed

---

[48] WCR to Sophie, July 17, 1863, William C. Russel Correspondence, Duke University.
[49] F. L. Higginson to WCR, July 21, 1863 (Duke University).

to be well, but it was impossible to get him off at the time & a few minutes afterwards the remains of the regiment were driven back.

I think Cabot is a prisoner & probably shot in the leg, as he seems to have been unable to walk. I hope we shall hear something more in a few days through a flag of truce which will probably be sent in.

Cabot fell doing his best to lead his company on & was almost on top of the parapet when struck. Our regiment did as finely as any men could do, but the support, as is usual in such cases, failed & the fire was so fearfully hot that it was impossible to withstand it – men who have been through all the Virginia & Maryland battles said they had never seen anything that approached it. The regiment lost one half of all the men who went in & a much larger proportion of officers.

F. L. Higginson

Shortly after receiving this letter, William Russel traveled to South Carolina and attempted to find his son. He met with Frank Higginson and they interviewed "a rebel boy that was in Fort Wagner at the time." The boy related finding two soldiers – one on top of the other – one alive and one dead. He carried the wounded man into the fort and he was not expected to live as he was bleeding badly. Based on the young man's description of the wounded soldier, Russel determined it must have been Cabot. He wrote, "…his fate is nearly decided in my mind…"[50]

---

[50] WCR letter c. July 1863 (Duke University).

Russel's hope that Cabot may have survived and was being held prisoner was raised after he met with a Lieut. Taylor who was injured on top of the parapet in the same battle and had returned to New York. He told Russel he heard that two officers of the 54th Regiment were being held prisoner and believed one of them to be Cabot.[51]

Spurred by Taylor's words of encouragement, William wrote to Brig. General Quincy A. Gillmore asking him to contact the Confederate Commanding General in Charleston to inquire whether Cabot was "in his possession."[52] A New York newspaper account was less encouraging, "Both these young men (Jackson & Simpkins) were thus left in the hands of the rebels, and of their fate we are left in painful uncertainty."[53]

Meanwhile, Matilda Russel contacted the hospital that treated the wounded after the battle but there was no record of Cabot having been there.[54] Brigadier General Thomas Jordan of the Confederate States Army wrote to Russel that "no officer of the 54th Massachusetts /colored/ Regiment has been found among the prisoners captured in the operations against Charleston."[55] Apparently not willing to totally accept Jordan's statement, William wrote to his late wife's sister of his concern that Cabot was or had been held prisoner by the Confederate Army, "If I could only know that Cabot died in

---

[51] WCR to Lucy, August 3, 1863 (Duke University).

[52] WCR to Q. A. Gilmore (sic), Aug. 7, 1863 (Duke University).

[53] *The Evening Post*, c. August 12, 1863 (Duke University).

[54] F. M. Robertson to Matilda Russel, Sept. 8th, 1863 (Duke University).

[55] (Brig. Gen'l Thomas Jordan to WCR, September 14, 1863 (Duke University).

the fair conduct of a battle I should feel very easy. But there was so much that was sweet in him that the suspicion of cruelty and unfair advantage taken of him is very hard to bear."[56]

Death seemed to surround William Russel. He had struggled for three months with the uncertainty of Cabot's survival. In October 1863, his father died and in mid-November his mother passed from this life as well. Russel's research into spiritualism never seemed to re-surface after the events at the house on East 27th. Perhaps he had drawn conclusions discounting the ability of the living to communicate with the dead, or perhaps it was now too painful to attempt to communicate and risk failure and disappointment.

Russel began to move on with his life. Whether he was despondent over Cabot's loss and the loss of his parents or had some sort of personal enlightenment, it is uncertain. But soon after the reality of Cabot's death set in, our man Russel gave up his law practice of nearly thirty years and moved his family far away from the busy streets of New York.

---

[56] WCR to Ellen, October 8, 1863 (Duke University).

Another Experiment

When William Russel journeyed to the South to try to either find his son or recover his remains, he was "appalled by pathetic and deplorable conditions in that socially-disoriented, war-torn area."[57] Russel was no ordinary man; he was a man who lived up to his convictions. Distraught, though not depressed, he attempted to direct his energies into helping the plight of the recently emancipated black slaves.

Early in 1864, he uprooted his wife and family from New York and moved to Tennessee to participate in a Reconstruction experiment at the Childress Plantation near Murfreesboro. In better days, that plantation witnessed the marriage of one of its daughters to a young lawyer named James Polk, who would become president of the United States in 1844.

Russel worked to provide a system whereby freed slaves would work on the plantation, grow cotton, and receive wages for doing so. His daughter Lucy appears to have been teaching the children of the workers as well as her own brother and sister.

In several letters[58] to Ellen Jackson of Boston (William's first wife's sister), Lucy and William wrote of some of the hardships living in Tennessee including the uncomfortable heat, lack of meat, being hassled by Confederate troops in the area. The war was still underway though the area around Murfreesboro was heavily occupied by Union troops. In one

---

[57] Hewett, 30-31.
[58] William C. Russel Correspondence, Duke University.

letter,[59] Lucy expressed concerns about what her father was doing in Tennessee. She wrote:

> "…(this work) certainly endangers his life somewhat because he felt the right way to destroy slavery was for northern men to settle here & try this experiment. The little spice of danger makes the work pleasant. I don't think that the Father of so many little children has much right to try such experiments, but with that I have nothing to do."

Russel's experiment lasted just over a year. It isn't clear what motivated Russel to give up his activities at Childress Plantation. Whether it was pressure from his family, the end of the war and the formalization of reconstruction activities by the government, financial considerations or something else, he relocated his family once again.

In 1865, William Channing Russel moved his family to Yellow Springs, Ohio and proceeded to join the faculty and board of trustees at Horace Mann's Antioch College. There he lectured in the Department of Metaphysical, Moral and Political Science for two years and was a trustee of the college.

His stay there was short-lived and in early 1867, Russel became the first professor of modern languages and adjunct-professor of history at the newly opened Cornell University in Ithaca, New York. Andrew Dickson White, President of Cornell, stated "Into all of his work he brought a perfect loyalty to truth, with the trained faculties of a lawyer in

---

[59] Lucy C. Russel to Aunt Ellen, Murfreesboro, May 8, 1864 (Duke University).

seeking it and the fearlessness of an apostle in announcing it."[60]

In 1870, Russel was appointed Vice-President of Cornell and remained in the administration of the college until 1881 when he resigned. He moved to Providence, Rhode Island for a brief teaching stint (1881-1883) as Acting Professor of History and Political Economy at Brown University and shortly thereafter retired to Yonkers, New York. His second wife Matilda pre-deceased him in 1876 and this spirited man passed into the other world on February 24, 1896.

---

[60] Andrew Dickson White, 436-437.

Afterword

My search for William Russel has come to an end. Fortunately, he left enough of his writings scattered about the country to help me round out his life and understand this one-time ghost hunter and seeker of spiritual knowledge. Certainly, one reason he became so interested in spirit matters was due to his incessant drive for intellectual improvement and his belief that the mind continues to be improved in the afterlife. But there was, perhaps, a more powerful personal motivation that drove him to pursue his investigation beyond the specific events at 107 East 27th Street - the emptiness he suffered after the death of his beloved wife Sarah. At the time of her death, Russel wrote a letter to her sister Hannah. Within his words we gain an even greater understanding of this sensitive man.

August 26, 1844

"Dear Hannah,

...Earth has no words to express the depth and meaning, the full sweep and power of such events. I try to talk of her and silence alone says what I have to say, and if I do speak, I only express the uppermost lightest feeling of the heart. I cannot make another feel my relation to her. No one who has not himself been ingrown with another being so long that she has become a part of his life, of his habits, of his thinking, feeling, struggling, falling, rising, of all his sufferings here and his hopes of the hereafter, can understand what the separation is.

I myself do not realize it. My heart often indulges in the belief that it is all a dream, and at times the mention of her name wakes no other feeling than it always did. Her annual absence seems to have taken place as usual and I cannot conceive that she will not return. I am certain the extent – the dreadful depth that separates us – the utter loneliness to which she has left me have never yet been fully understood. How then make another understand it?

My only wish for you is that you may be happy while you can. Be truly happy in the present. Give up living for the future, or caring for the future. Insure your true happiness now…Be happy now in the love that is around you and leave the future for the love that will await you. If I had enjoyed the passing time more, I would have made Sarah happier. If I had done that, my present grief would be more selfish and less poignant. If we were to live more for one another, we should be doing the most for ourselves…"[61]

So this is William Russel – Columbia graduate, successful lawyer, loving husband, spiritual investigator, distraught father, active abolitionist, college professor and insightful philosopher. Perhaps, in a manner of speaking, Mr. Russel himself has communicated with us from the "other side." No medium to assist; no dim lights; no unnerving spirit rappings; no vague, scrawled messages…just Russel's highly personal letter, written in his own hand. His heartfelt words about living more for one another have crossed the barriers of death and time, and his message to us is ageless.

---

[61] WCR to Hannah Jackson, August 26, 1844. William C. Russel Papers, Cornell University.

References

Britten, Emma Hardinge. *Two Worlds*. November 18, 1887.

Burchard, Peter. *One Gallant Rush: Robert Gould Shaw & His Brave Black Regiment*. NY: St. Martin's Press, 1965.

Catalogue of the Officers and Students of Brown University 1881-82. Providence: J.A. & R.A. Reid, 1881.

Catalogue of the Officers and Students of Brown University 1882-83. Providence: J.A. & R.A. Reid, 1882.

Channing, William F. *The Fire-Alarm Telegraph: A Lecture Delivered before the Smithsonian Institution, March, 1855*. Boston: Redding & Company, 1855.

Christian Inquirer. New York: Unitarian Association of the State of New York, 15 November, 1862.

The Cornellian. Ithaca: The Secret Societies, 1870 – 1882.

Encyclopedia Britannica. Cambridge, England: University Press, 1911, 11th edition.

Emilio, Luis F. *A Brave Black Regiment*. Boston: The Boston Book Company, 1894.

Flammarion, Camille. *Mysterious Psychic Forces*. Boston: Small, Maynard and Company, 1907.

Greeley, Horace. *Recollections of a Busy Life*. Miami: Mnemosyne Publishing, 1969. (originally printed in 1868).

Hardinge, Emma. *Modern American Spiritualism: a twenty years' record of the communion between earth and the world of spirits*. New Hyde Park: University Books, 1970. (originally printed in 1870).

Hewett, Waterman Thomas. *Cornell University: A History*. New York: University Publishing Society, 1905.

Keller, Dorothy Jean. *A Study of William Channing Russel as First Vice-President and Acting President of Cornell University, 1870 – 1880*. Thesis for Master of Arts, Cornell University, 1961.

Mitchell, Martha. *Encyclopedia Brunoniana*. Providence: Brown University Library, 1993.

New York Evening Post, December 12, 1853. (WCR marriage)

New York Times, 24 November 1862, p. 5. (Carrenos Concert)

New York Times, 6 January 1862, p. 5. (Menzies Obituary)

New York Times, 7 April 1874, p. 8. (Judge Edmonds' Obituary)

New York Times, 25 February 1896.

Photograph of William Channing Russel by William Frear. Faculty Biographical Files. Division of Rare and Manuscript Collections, Cornell University Library.

Russel, William C. *Address and Poem before the Association of the Alumni of Columbia College, November 13th, 1861.* New York: The Ass'n of the Alumni of Columbia College, 1861.

Russel, William C. Correspondence 1856 - 1865. Duke University, Rubenstein Library.

Russel, William C. *Education and Character. An Address Delivered before the Delta Upsilon Fraternity, at Amherst, Mass., May 28, 1873.* Amherst: Henry M. Cloud, 1874.

Russel, William C. *Memoranda of Examinations of the Phenomenon of "Spiritualism."* Original manuscript written 1862-1863. Author's collection.

Russel, William C. Papers. Archives 3-2-2292, Cornell University Library, Division of Rare and Manuscript Collections.

Russel, William C. *To the Honorable the Common Council of the City of New York. The Memorial of William C. Russel, of the City of New York, respectfully represents…Patents for the American Fire Alarm Telegraph...*New York, 1854.

Selkreg, John H. (ed.) *Landmarks of Tomkins County New York.* Syracuse: D. Mason, 1894.

Thomas, Milton Halsey. *Columbia University Officers and Alumni 1754 – 1857.* Morningside Heights: Columbia University Press, 1936.

Underhill, Leah. *The Missing Link in Modern Spiritualism.* NY: Arno Press, 1976. (originally printed in 1885).

Unidentified Medium's Manuscript Notebook, 1859 - 1869. Author's collection.

White, Andrew Dickson. *Autobiography of Andrew Dickson White.* New York: The Century Co., 1905.